Wordpress for Beginners

A Step by Step Guide for Quickly and Easily Designing a Beautiful Website from Scratch in 2018 (Contains 2 Texts – Wordpress for Beginners & SEO)

WordPress for Beginners

A Step-by-Step Guide to Building Your Own WordPress Website from Scratch in 2018

Table of Contents

About the Author

Mark Williams is website professional who has used WordPress in many of his projects over the years. While he has dabbled a bit in coding and enjoys learning about new things in the world of technology, his passion is to help others learn how to work online. Williams enjoys creating websites, working on social media, and helping his clients develop the best projects to help their business improve and to increase sales. While there are many other great website builders out there, Williams believes that WordPress is one of the best available for most businesses because you don't need to be an expert to create an expert website.

Introduction

Congratulations on downloading your personal copy of *WordPress for Beginners: A Step-by-Step Guide to Building Your Own WordPress Website from Scratch in 2018.* Thank you for doing so.

The following chapters will discuss some of the many great things that you are able to do with your website, all with the help of WordPress. We will start from the very beginning by looking at what WordPress really is and how you will be able to find your own domain name and hosting site, then utilize WordPress to have an easy to manage website that does exactly what you need it to. WordPress is one of the most widely used systems online because it really makes it easy to manage any kind of website that you want.

In addition to getting some of the basics in place such as installing WordPress and getting the hosting and domain name, we will look at some of the other important things that you will need when it comes to making your own website with WordPress. We will explore how to pick out and install a theme, the importance of working with widgets and plugins to increase functionality on the website, how to create a page and a post, creating your own menus, keeping your website secure on WordPress, and even how to track the analytics on how well the website is doing.

While there may be other sites out there that can help you manage your web presence, none of them have as many features or the benefits that come with WordPress. Make sure to check out this guidebook and learn some of the basics that you need to know to get started on creating your own website today!

There are plenty of books on this subject on the market, thanks again for choosing this one! Every effort was made to ensure it is full of as much useful information as possible. Please enjoy!

Chapter 1: What is WordPress

Many businesses and individuals are excited about building their own websites. They want to be able to create their own personal page, somewhere that they can sell their products or reach out to others who may need to contact them. A business can use this as a landing page to attract customers to their store, or to sell some of their services. Students use these websites to make portfolios to impress future employers; authors can place their books online to sell, and many people start up their own blogs, writing articles about things that are important to them. There are many different reasons why people would choose to start their own websites and there are luckily a lot of options that come with building a website so that each person can get exactly what they need.

But before we start working on building a new website with the help of WordPress, we need to have a good idea what this site is. To start, WordPress is a content management system, or a CMS, which is basically a system that you can use to manage all the content of your website. Without the help of a CMS, the website owner would need to learn how to do coding on their own or find a developer who could alter their source code whenever they wanted to make changes on any of their pages.

Learning how to code to make a few simple changes or to create your own page in the first place can take a lot of time and effort, but programs like WordPress take some of the work out of it. In fact, you can use WordPress for your website without having any coding knowledge.

But there is a lot more that WordPress is able to do to help you out. In addition to helping you to manage your own website, it is going to provide you with an actual framework for your website. WordPress is able to take care of all the groundwork that comes with building your website. Then the user, which in this case is you, can come in and make any customizations that they would like to their personal website. WordPress is really easy to use, so even beginners are able to design the web page that they want.

Now, there are a few different ways that you can use WordPress, but in this guidebook, we are going to concentrate on self-hosting on this site. This is basically when you are going to download your own files and folders from WordPress.org so that you can have your own hosting and a bit more freedom. You may have heard about WordPress.com, but with this one, you would only use it if you want WordPress the company to host the website instead of finding your own hosting provider like Bluehost or Siteground.

There is nothing wrong with using WordPress to help with hosting in the beginning, but the name of your website is not going to look as professional. With this one, you will be getting a URL that looks like "yourdomain.wordpress. com". If you are a business or a professional, having the WordPress part in the picture is not going to look that great, so it is often best to work with WordPress.org's CMS files and use your own hosting and domain name. There are many features that are available with WordPress.org that aren't present in the other dependently-hosted versions, so for making your own professional website, the self-hosted version of WordPress is often the best choice for you.

Using WordPress to build a website

WordPress is a highly used system all around the world. It is estimated that almost a fourth of the websites that are currently active use WordPress in some manner because it is so easy to work with and provides a lot of different options. Once you decide that you like the features of WordPress and you want to start building your own website, it is time to get going.

Depending on the means that you used to come across WordPress, you probably used WordPress.org and downloaded and installed the whole thing, just to find out that when you clicked on the download button, you ended up with a lot of folders and files, with no idea what you should do with all of them.

In order to understand more about WordPress and what these files all mean, we first need a better understanding of how a website works. All of the websites that are available online today will come with three basic parts. They are going to have a domain (which you can pick out), they have some kind of hosting account, and they have the code for the website. For the website to work, all of these things need to be linked together. You will need to provide the code for the website, but you can purchase the hosting account and the domain name.

When you go through and purchase a hosting account, you basically rent out a part of a server. To keep things simple, we are going to treat the spot that you rented out on the server like space on the Internet, so you basically are renting out some real estate online. The hosting provider is the land that the website would be sitting on while the domain could be the address, but you can pick out what address you would like to give your website so that others are able to find it a bit easier.

This is simplifying the whole process a little bit, but it helps to show the importance of having all the parts there. So basically, the website that you are creating is just a bunch of code that is put together into folders and files, all of which will sit on a server which the public is able to access (you want them to be able to access it or they will never be able to find your website). For most people who don't know how to do coding, one of the hardest parts of building their website is figuring out how to write up all the code that will make these files so that the website works. This is where WordPress can step in and help.

WordPress is set up by way of folders and files that were premade and that can be used to make up your websites' foundation, complete with all of the stuff that you will need to start customizing and building the website. This is great for the beginner, because it means that they do not need to build up every folder and file of their website on their own. This is why WordPress is so valuable: it allows anyone who has a computer and some knowledge of this site to create their own website and to make changes to that website without having to know coding or hiring an expensive web developer to help them get it done. Putting the power in your own hands to get the work done, especially if it is something as simple as writing your own blog, can be really valuable to many WordPress users.

Purchasing your domain and hosting

So, as we discussed a bit above, before you start using WordPress to create your site, you need to go through and do a few other steps. First, you need to purchase the domain name that you would like to use. Make sure that you go with one that is professional and sounds right for your business. Then you will need to purchase your hosting from a company that you trust and like. Sometimes, you can find both the domain name and the hosting offered through one company so this can make things easier.

There are two methods that you can use in order to purchase the domain and the hosting. The first one is to purchase the domain and your hosting through the same company. This is the easiest way to get started and will save you a few steps along the way.

The second method is to purchase your domain name with one company and then go and get the hosting through another. This one is often used if you already have your domain name ready but you don't have an account for hosting. Sometimes you would just rather purchase the domain name from one place and then do the hosting through another.

Purchasing domain and hosting together

If you are going to purchase the domain and the hosting together, you need to find a company that offers this feature. Many of the modern hosting sites will offer you the domain and the hosting together so this shouldn't be a big deal, but take some time to look around at each of the sites and see if they offer everything that you would like and if they are easy for you to use.

Once you have decided on the hosting provider that you want to use, it is time for you to make the purchase. To purchase these both through the same company, you need to go to the hosting provider that you want to use (such as Bluehost) and then click so that you end up on their hosting page. This should be pretty easy to find. You just need to go to their main navigation, which is often at the top of their website, and then you should see "Hosting" or some variation on this. For this part, stick with the most basic hosting option available because you can always check it out and make changes later.

If you have an idea of the domain name that you want to use, you can search for it here, or you can type in some keywords that go with your website theme and see what domain names are available for you to pick with. GoDaddy is a good one to search through in order to find what domain names are available, even if you don't choose to use them for your hosting. Namecheckr.com is a good one because it not only checks to see if the domain name is available but it will show if anyone has taken that name for social media channels so you can start your branding off right.

The good news is that if you purchase the hosting and the domain name together, you should get the domain for free, so don't purchase it yet. Once you find the domain that you would like to use, go back to the "Hosting" section in the hosting provider that you picked and then select which plan is the best for you. You will then be able to go through the process, add in the domain name that you want, and finish out the process with a good domain name and hosting.

Purchasing the domain and hosting separately

In some cases, you may already have your domain name and will need to get a hosting company. This is when you will need to change the name servers, the parts that will point your domain to the hosting account so that when your customers type in your domain, it will pull up your website.

This option can take more time because the domain address needs to be linked up to whatever hosting that you pick later on and it often takes some coding and a few more steps than you may be ready to handle as a beginner. Often it is best to just purchase the two together because this saves a lot of time and avoids some confusion.

When it comes to creating your own website, it can be confusing to make sure that all the parts are together, especially if you are a beginner and don't know what is going on. With the help of WordPress, and picking out your own domain name and hosting, you will be able to create a great site for your business or personal use.

Chapter 2: Installing WordPress

Now that you have taken the time to get your domain name and hosting and you set up the basic account with WordPress, it is time to install this onto your computer. There are two methods that you are able to use in order to install the WordPress system.

The easiest method to do this is to let the WordPress installer application get it done. Your hosting account should provide this to you and this can make it almost a seamless experience to get both of them hooked up together. For this to work, you simply need to log onto the hosting account and look for the link to your hosting account control panel (this can be in the cPanel, or there may be a link that says something like "manage hosting account").

- Once you are in here, you will be able to look for the WordPress installer application. Inside of your hosting, it will most likely just be the WordPress logo with the words WordPress with it. This is an application that has been designed with the idea of making the installation of

17

WordPress on your server easier. All that you will need to do now in order to get WordPress installed on the computer is:

- Open up the application for the WordPress installer

- Tell it which domain you are going to install WordPress on

- Make sure that you leave the Directory field blank (it will probably say blog by default so make sure to unclick that)

- Enter the login and password

- Click to install

It should only take a few minutes to install and then you will see a prompt that says that the WordPress install is ready to go. You will then be able to jump right in and get started on the new website. It really can be as simple as that!

There is another method to use if you need, that includes installing WordPress directly to your computer rather than to the hosting server, but it is really hard for a beginner to get down and since the other method is easy to work with, that is the one that most people are going to choose to simplify the whole process.

What is on the dashboard

If you haven't had a chance to log onto the WordPress website, it is now time to do this. You just need to type in the domain name into the address bar of whatever browser you want to use, making sure to add in the "/wp-admin" with it, and then hit enter. You should now see a login form where you can type in the username and the password that you created when you were installing WordPress. Once you are done logging in, you should be sent right to the dashboard in WordPress. You will see a menu that is on the left side of the screen and then there are also some boxes on the right. These boxes that are to the right will show things like news and activity and basically an overhead look at the site. But the left side is full of a lot of tabs and buttons that you will want to learn how to use. On this side, you will see many items like Pages, Media, Posts, and Dashboard. There are many things that you can do with the menu options on the left, but we will talk about just a few of them to keep things brief.

Some of the main points that are going to be on the dashboard, and that you will probably use often, include:

- Posts: this is the section that you will use when you want to create a new post, such as when writing your own blog. Posts are usually going to have a time stamp on them and then can be organized into different categories.

- Pages: this is where you are able to create some new pages for the site, like a Contact Us page or an About Us page. These are the static pages where there isn't going to be any time specifications with them and you won't need to categorize them like the posts. This can include the landing page, the thank you page, and more.

- Media: if you want to add things like PDFs, videos, and pictures to the mix, you will be able to add them to the site and edit them in the Media section.

- Appearance: this is where you are able to change your theme, customize the website, create some navigation menus, add in widgets, and so much more.

- Plugins: this section will allow you to search as well as install some new plugins for the site. These Plugins are basically like the apps that you will use with WordPress.

- Tools: this is what you will use when you want to bring in content from another WordPress site or if you are trying to export your site's content. This is useful if you are switching domains or moving the website for some reason.

- Settings: there are many parts of the Settings tab that you can deal with, including General, Writing, Reading, Discussion, and more.

If you are new to working with WordPress, it may be a good idea to take some time and mess around on the dashboard so that you can learn how this whole thing works. There are many great features and tasks that you can do on the WordPress site, you just need to find where all of the stuff is and get to work!

Chapter 3: Creating a "Coming Soon" Page

During the time that you are creating your website, your domain is live and there are some people who know about your business who will try to get on the website. But it is best to release the website altogether, finished, rather than just pieces of it. This helps it to look professional and will better show off your business. In the meantime, you may want to add in a "Coming Soon" page so that your customers aren't able to get onto the unfinished page, but they still know that your website domain name is correct.

To get started, we are going to install our first plugin. We will talk about the Plugins a bit later on, but for now, we are going to use the plugin that comes from SeedProd and is known as the Coming Soon Page and Maintenance Mode.

To get started, you will need to find the Plugins menu item, which should be on the left side of the dashboard in WordPress. Then you can click on Add New, which is at the top of your screen. There should be a search bar at the top right of the page and you can type in "coming soon" before hitting enter. The SeedProd option should be one of the first options on the list so go ahead and click on it.

Once this plugin is installed into the WordPress page, you can head over to the settings of this plugin to make sure everything is working the way that you would like. You just need to hover over the "Settings" that are on the left of the dashboard and then click on "Coming Soon Page and Maintenance Mode". At the top section in this setting, you should see that it is disabled by default. You can select to Enable this mode and then click to save the changes.

Scroll down a bit on the page and you should see that it is possible to upload your logo, add in the heading that you would like, and even add in a new message. You can add in any of the messages that you would like into here, but keep it professional. Something like, "Our new website is coming soon. Check back later!" would work just fine for the message that you would like to leave. In some cases, the business likes to leave contact information, like a phone number or a business email so that your customers have a way to reach you if it is needed while you are working on the website.

At this point, you can scroll down that page a little bit and click on the "Save All Changes". When this is done, you should be all done with the setup. This is really all that you would need for the Coming Soon page at this point. It is enough to let other people know that you are working on the page, even though they aren't able to get on it right now, and allows them a chance to get ahold of you if needed.

Now, you can also get a little more creative with what you would like to do with this Coming Soon page. You can scroll to the top of this plugin and work on the Design tab as well. This is a great way to change some of the elements that are on this new page, such as the text color, changing up the background, adding in some images, and other things to show off the Coming Soon page more if you would like.

As a beginner, keeping the Coming Soon page pretty simple is the best option for you to do. This allows you to keep the customers away from the website while you are working on it and keeping it simple will save some of that creative energy for when you need to start working on the actual website.

Chapter 4: Installing a Theme and Working on Your First Pages and Posts

So now that the Coming Soon page is all set up to keep things organized, it is time to get started on working on the real website. You want to make it look nice and neat to really convince the customers that you a legitimate business and ready to take things on. One of the first things that you should do in order to get the website set up is to install a theme for your WordPress website. There are many possibilities that you can choose from with your theme and you can decide the type of design and the complexity that comes with the theme that works the best for you. You can make your own, have someone make one for you, or choose to pick from the ones that are available through WordPress.

If you choose to go with a WordPress theme that is already available, you will find that there are two routes that you can take. You can choose to go with the free themes, or you can choose one of the premium themes.

The free themes can easily be found inside of the theme directory for WordPress. To find this directory, you just need to get onto your dashboard or WordPress and then hover over the Appearance before clicking on Themes. You will be able to see a list of all the themes that you have already installed on the system and then you can click on the button for "Add New" to get to the theme directory.

From here, you will be able to filter out the different themes that are available based on different categories, such as subject, features, layout, and colors. If you want to get a closer look at what one of the themes looks like, you just need to click on the Preview button or click on the image. Once you have found one that you think looks nice or works with the kind of website that you are creating, you will just need to click on Install it. After the installation is all done, you must make sure that you Activate the theme so that it will be ready for you to make changes to.

After this is done, you may wonder why the theme doesn't look exactly like the one that you picked when you were in the directory. This is because the theme designer is going to build out the themes with pages, images, certain settings, menus, and posts so that it is easier to showcase. Since you just downloaded the theme and haven't changed any of the settings or added any pages, the theme is not going to look exactly as you would expect right now.

You should take the time to really pick out a good theme. There are some themes that are going to work out better than others, but in some cases, they are really complicated and the only way that you will be able to get the theme to match on your website is to manually go through the code. This can take quite a bit of time if the theme isn't set up well. Other themes are going to have theme options that you can find on the admin dashboard or you can go to the Appearance tab and click on Customize. Every theme is going to be a bit different, but the ones that are good will make it easy to customize what is going on with the site and you won't have to learn how to read the code to make the changes that you want. Not only does the right theme help to make your website look more professional and attract customers, it also helps you to have an easier time creating the page.

The premium themes

It is also possible to pick out one of the premium themes that are available through WordPress. These ones are going to cost you a bit of money (the exact amount is going to vary depending on where you get them and some of the features that you need) and they are going to be found outside of the theme directory. These often have a higher quality to them, have more choices n design, and you will usually get some support help when needed.

Almost any situation and website type will benefit from using a premium theme. The free themes can be nice for some blogs or for starting out if you get them from a developer who is reliable, but if you want to have something that is more unique to your website or you want a better design to help your site look more professional, the premium themes are going to give you the right results.

There are many companies that will sell some of these premium themes including StudioPress and Themeforest.net. You should look through both of these to get some ideas of what premium themes are available and to see if there are some that you like for your website. You can also look through some other options and there are so many available that you are sure to find the one that matches up with what your website needs.

The process for installing one of these premium themes will be different than working with the free themes since you are getting them outside of the WordPress site. Once you purchase the premium theme that you want to use, you will receive a .zip file from whatever company you purchased it from. This is the file that you will need to use in order to install the theme for your site. Once you get that file downloaded onto the computer, it is time to go to the dashboard for WordPress, hover over the Appearance part, and then click on Themes. You should see the Add New button at the top and you should click on it.

Now that you are here, you can click on the "Upload theme" button that is near the top and then make sure that you click on "Choose File". You will need to look through your files to find the one for your theme and then click on "Open" before clicking on "Install Now". When that is done installing, click the activate link and now the premium theme should live. You will be ready to use that theme to make the different pages that you need in WordPress and to get the website up and running.

Creating your pages and posts

While picking out the theme is really important, so far you just have some empty pages sitting there and nothing would show up if you posted the website live right now. You need to add some posts and some pages, as well as some other options, onto the page to share information, sell products, or to get other things done with your website. One thing that can be confusing for some people in WordPress is that there are differences between posts and pages.

With posts, you are publishing something that is going to have a time stamp put on them. They are syndicated through the RSS feeds, which means that people are able to subscribe to these posts and will get an update whenever you publish a new post. They will allow you to put in a comments section so that others can start a discussion and they are often going to be listed in reverse chronological order on the blog so that the newer posts are on the top.

Often, posts are going to be used when you want to start a blog or add in some news and other information (such as press releases) to your website. This allows you to keep your page to the top of SEO and can make it easier to write your articles without making them permanent.

Pages are going to be a bit different. These are static pages, like the welcome page, the contact us page, and so on. They are not going to be time specific and they will not have any syndication through the RSS feeds. They will also not be included in the blog feed.

How to add a post

First, we are going to add a post. To do this, go to the dashboard of WordPress and then click on the "Posts" page in the menu. You can then click on the "Add New" part that is near the top. At this location, you will be able to enter the title that you would like before clicking on your text editor, which should be right below your title. It should only take a few seconds, but you should be able to see the URL for your post come right under the title that you added. You can click on Edit if you would like to change it.

The text editor is where you will be able to add in the content that you would like. There are lots of tools at the top of the text editor that are similar to the ones that you see on Microsoft Word so that you can bold, italicize, make words bigger, and do other things to the text that you add inside.

When you are all done with the post, you should see a box that says Publish. You will see a Preview button and a Save Draft button that is at the top of this button. There are also options for Status as well as Visibility and all of them will allow you to make edits to them. You can change this to Pending or Draft at any time or you can make it public if you want to publish this post online for others to see. If you are doing a simple blog post, you could just click on Publish immediately and this will get it ready to go online.

Now, before you let this post go online, it is a good idea to add some tags and some categories for it. At this point, we haven't gone through and created any of the categories for it yet, so it is going to be labeled as Uncategorized here. You can add in some of the categories that you would like to give this post as well as some tags. Take some time to get this done to help organize and to make it easier for others to see the posts when searching on this topic.

Adding a Featured Image is a good idea as well, because it increases the visibility of the post and kind of gives a better idea of what this post is about. Each of the themes that you can pick will decide when and how to use the featured image. Try out a sample one to see how it is going to look in the theme, but make sure to change it before publishing to make the post look better.

Adding a page

The process for adding and then editing a page will be similar to what we did for adding posts, which may be why there is some confusion. You just need to click on the "Pages" button that is on your dashboard and then click the "Add New" that is at the top. Many of the options on this will be the same as with the posts, but there won't be options to add in tags and categories. You will also notice that there is a "Page Attributes" box to the right side when you are editing a page. This is where you would assign things like a parent page if you want to add in services and then have pages under that one for each of the services.

Make sure that you think through all of the pages that you would like to add into your WordPress site. These are going to influence what the website will look like and can determine if the site turns out the way that you want. Each business will have different things inside of it depending on their needs, but options like a Welcome page, Services Offered, About Us page, and a Contact Us page can all be useful when dealing with the layout of your page.

Chapter 5: Create a Navigation Menu

At this point, you should have created a few of the pages that you want for your website. Once there are at least two or more pages available on the website, it is time to create a new menu for the site. This will make it easier for your customers to be able to find the pages that they need inside of WordPress. To get started on this, you will need to hover over Appearance and then click on Menus.

From this location, you will give the menu a name and then click on the button that says "create menu". Now you will be able to start adding the items that you would like into the menu. You will notice to the left side that you can use various tools like custom links, categories, posts, and pages to create your menu. You just need to check the boxes next to the categories or the pages that you would like to add to the menu. When you have picked an item that you would like to add, just click on the button for Add to Menu. Once they are added to the menu, you can always click and drag these items around so that you can get them into the order that you want.

Now, it is pretty easy to create these navigation menus, but we are going to go over a few things about the menus to make sure that you are able to create the perfect one.

Sub-menus

A sub-menu is going to basically be a menu that is nested within another menu item. For example, if you had a menu item and you want to put some sub-categories into this menu item, you would make them into a nested menu. This does sound a little bit confusing at first, but let's say that you have a menu item that is the category of services offered. You can then make sub-menus for all of the services that you want to offer such as advertising, branding, market research, SEO, sales, and so on.

To get a new submenu started inside of WordPress, you would first just need to add in all of the items that you want for the sub-menu. When they are all in there, just grab the items and drag them so that they are underneath but then slightly to the right of the menu item that you would like to get them nested under. If you did this right, you should see that all of these nested items that are in the same sub-menu will be aligned and they are going to be just right of the parent menu item.

Now you will need to save the work and then click on refresh. Now you should notice that your nested items in the menu are only going to show up if you hover over the parent item in the menu.

Custom links

The next thing that we need to work on is custom links. Let's say that we want to work on a new item in the menu that is called Services. When this is added, you can then add in the sub-menu items for each service that you offer. For this exercise, though, we are going to say that we don't really have a Services page that will list all of your services. Instead, we have different landing pages for all of the services and you would like to make sure that the visitors will go directly to these landing pages for whatever service they are interested in.

To get this to happen, you will need to learn how to add a custom link to the menu, making sure that the text of the link is "Services". The URL shouldn't be empty at this point, so for now, you can just put in the "#" or "/" to keep it simple.

As soon as you are done adding in the menu item, you will need to click on it to start editing. Delete the URL that is there and click on save. Now you should have a menu item that isn't really a link, but instead, it has become a parent menu item that will take visitors to the right item in the sub-menu, which in this case is going to be the services of your business.

One last step

This is an important step because if you end up missing out on it, you will be stuck and not know how to make the menus show up on your site. You should notice that under the Menu Settings, there is a button for "Theme Locations". These are the locations that are set up by the theme that you picked out, and if you check on one of the boxes that are located here, it will tell your theme where you would like to place this menu. If you don't take the time to assign a location to your menu, it is not going to show up on the website.

Most developers create certain locations in their theme where they would like the menu to show up. For the most part, these are going to be in the footer or the header, but in other cases, there are some themes that get creative and will include it in other locations. Play around a bit to see where the menu ends up each time that you check a box and which area looks the best for your website.

Creating a menu can make it easier to work with your website and helps your customers to get around the page much easier than before. You can mess around to help the menu work the way that you want based on what is inside of your website, but try to keep it pretty simple so that your customers can navigate around the site easily.

Chapter 6: Working with the Widgets and Sidebars

In all of the WordPress themes that you find, there are areas that are known as "widget areas". These can sometimes be called sidebars as well so you may hear them by that name as well, but they are going to be the same thing. Widget areas are the areas that will display your widgets; widgets are the blocks of content that will display some of the added features on the website.

Let's look at it a different way. Your phone has some different apps on it that do different things. You could have an app for getting on Facebook and some apps for taking notes and so much more. The widgets are going to be like apps for the website. Each of these widgets will be able to do a different task and each of them has their own purpose. For example, there are some widgets that are good for displaying text, some of displaying the categories that you can use, and some that will display your recent posts, and so on.

But these widgets, even though they can do quite a bit for your website, can only be placed on the page in certain areas. Usually, these are the areas that the developer of the theme created so that the widgets could be placed there. These will be known as the widget area. As long as you are keeping it in these areas, you can place any of the widgets in it, but you can't make a change to where the widget area is. So now that we know a bit more about the widgets, it is time to add the widgets into the right area of your website.

How to add widgets

When you are ready to find your own widgets, you need to hover over the Appearance tab on the dashboard and then click on the Widgets. There are many default widgets that are already found on WordPress to help you to create some of your own pages, and if you have already done some of the organizing of your web page, you will have had a chance to use them. Some of the default widgets that are found in WordPress include categories, pages, text, and search. If you would like to add one of these widgets over to the specific widget area, you just need to click on it and drag. You can also click the widget, select the area you wish to put it in, and then click on Add Widget.

Once you have placed the widget in the right area, you should be able to see some of the settings for it; you may need to click it to see some of these settings in some cases. Keep in mind that it is not required for a widget to have a setting so these may not have them, but they do have a title with them. Once the widget it in the right place on the page, you should be able to do a preview of the website and it will be displayed there. Unlike the other parts that you work with on the website, you will not find the traditional Save or Publish button.

One thing that may seem a little bit confusing is where these widget areas are inside of the theme and how you are able to move them. Every theme is going to have a different location for these widget areas and it is going to be based on where the developer placed it. You will not be able to move the widget area inside of WordPress without knowing how to code and being able to alter the code within your theme. For most beginners, this means that you will just need to deal with where the widget area is.

Create your own sidebars

Up to this point, we have just been adding in some of the widgets that are there by default in the WordPress dashboard. But you can also use some of your widgets in order to create a sidebar and we are even able to make the sidebar different for the pages and the sections that we are adding to the site. For example, you may want the sidebar of the Contact page to look a bit different than the sidebar that is on the Blog page.

There is a great plugin that you will be able to use that allows you to build and even customize sidebars on the various pages on the site. This plugin is called Custom Sidebars. To see how this particular plugin is going to work, we are going to create two sidebars, one for the Contact Page and one for the Blog page.

Now, we will need to open up the editor for these pages and on the right side you should see that there is an option to select a different sidebar for this page. We are going to select which sidebar we want to replace, and then we will click save. Now the new sidebar that we created is only going to show up on this page.

We can follow the same idea when we want to display different sidebars for certain post types or categories. You will find that there are quite a few ways to create as well as customize your sidebars, so take some time to explore around and make the changes that you would like. WordPress has made it pretty easy to move around the widgets, as long as you keep them in the widget area, and you just need to click the widget that you want and drag it around to make it work.

If you ever want to move one of the widgets that you have out of your sidebar or the other widget areas without having to delete it, you just need to drag it over to the section that is called "inactive widgets" so that it can be taken care of.

Widgets can do so many things inside of your website. They make it easier to add text and do other activities that make your page look amazing. You just need to pick which ones you would like to have available on each page, get them set up, and then see how they do on the website.

Chapter 7: The Basics of Plugins

We have talked a bit about what plugins are and which ones you will want to use for the various different parts of your website, but we haven't really taken the time to talk about what plugins are, how many of them you can use, and why you would necessarily want to use these on your page.

Plugins are actually one of the best features that are available inside of WordPress. These are basically ways to extend, as well as add to some of the functionality that is inside of WordPress. Plugins can also be seen as apps for the website just like widgets (because widgets are types of plugins) and there are many different plugins that you are able to choose from.

In order to get a new plugin into your WordPress website, you will need to download the one that you want and then install it, just like you would an app on your phone or your computer. Once you get the plugin installed, there are two methods that you can use in order to get it to display so that you can use it. One method that you can use is a method called shortcode. This is going to look like this:

[example-shortcode]

44

Plugins that use the shortcode will typically come with them so that you are able to copy and paste without having t worry about messing up while you are typing.

Another method that you can get the plugin to work is to use the widget to work with the plugin. You will need to keep the plugin in the widget area at all times, but it can be a great way to do this.

Let's take a look at an example of how you would do this. Let's say that you want to add in the contact form to your sidebar. You may notice that inside of your theme, there isn't already a widget for the contact form, so we are going to need to add in the plugin for this. To do this, click on the Plugins button on the left side of the dashboard and then you should be able to see a full list of any plugins that you already have installed in the system. We are not going to use these right now, rather, we are going to click on the Add New button that is on the top so that we can go to the plugin repository.

This repository is going to be like your theme directory when you want to get a free theme, but it will be for the plugins. These plugins are going to be free and they install similar to how we did earlier with themes. To find the one that we want, we will search in the repository for "contact form".

Here you should be able to see a list that includes the plugins for a contact form. You will be able to search through these to find the contact form that you would like to use. Here we are going to use Contact Form 7 so that is the name that we are going to look for here. When you find it, you can read through this to find out more information if needed.

Oftentimes, you will need to use the shortcode to get the plugin to work and each off the shortcodes for the plugin is going to be found in different places based on where the developer placed it. Some will have this shortcode present in the description, so make sure to take a look through this and copy it down for later. Others may put this information under the plugins Installation section. The Contact Form 7 is going to wait until after the form is created before giving you this shortcode, so we won't see this one in either of the two places. Shortcodes are sometimes hard to find, but you will need to find it in many cases if you would like to use the plugin.

Once you click on the Contact Form 7 option, you will need to install it and then look for where it is on the WordPress page. Each of the plugins is going to show up in different places inside of the dashboard so you may need to take some time to look for it. Sometimes you may find it on the Settings tab or the Tools app. Some will make it into a widget and sometimes you will notice that the plugin has its own tab. You may need to look around a bit to find it and get it all set up.

Contact Form 7 will create its own tab inside of the dashboard, which does make it a bit easier to find. Now you can go to this plugin, click on Add New, and then you can create a brand new form. Make the form pretty simple (you just need a bit of information for the customer to contact you), and then click on Save. Now that we have created this form, this plugin is going to give us the shortcode that is needed to make the form display (this is just for Contact Form 7, some of them show this earlier in the process).

You are able to use the shortcode that you are given anywhere that there is a text editor on the website. For example, you could copy this code and then head to your widgets section. Then drag over a text widget into the primary sidebar before pasting the shortcode and clicking save. Then the contact form would be there, once you click on refresh, on the sidebar that you created.

Sometimes the shortcode is going to be the hardest part about the plugins that you want to use because they are hard to find. There are many different places where they can be located and if you are not paying attention, you may miss out on them. A good thing to consider is to look through Google and see if you can find the shortcode if you happened to miss it.

There are many great plugins that you can add to your WordPress site and often the ones that you will pick depend on the information that you would like to use inside of your website. Here, we looked at how to add in the plugin for the contact us page, but you would use some of the same steps in order to make this work for other plugins as well. Take a look through some of the plugins that are part of the default of WordPress and look to see what others are available and see how they could enhance how well your website works.

Chapter 8: Securing Your Website

If you are making a website for your business, it is important to worry about the security that comes with the site. You don't want someone to get onto the website that you are working on and cause a lot of issues, spam your customers, and add other malicious things to the website. There are many reasons that a hacker would want to get onto your website. First WordPress is one of the most popular sites right now and there are thousands of websites that they are able to target. It is open source, so the code is available for anyone to mess around with and use. And most of the websites that go with WordPress are going to be third-party so this can add some vulnerabilities to the security of your code.

Keeping all of this in mind, it is a good idea to think about the security of your website early on so that you don't have deal with it when there is a big mess. The hacker just needs to find one vulnerability inside of your plugin or your theme and they can get onto the server and cause a lot of damage. Some of the things that you can do to make sure that your website is safe on WordPress include:

Keep things updated

Any time that your plugins, themes, and other things inside of WordPress are not up to date, it is easier for a hacker to get in. Updates are important because they change up the code a bit and some other things so that it is harder for a hacker to get in. You should check for updates in WordPress on a regular basis. You will be able to find this if you go to your dashboard in WordPress and click on Updates. After clicking on this, if you have an older version of WordPress or if there are some plugins that need to be updated, you can see and update them from here.

Pick a good username

Never make your username something that is easy to remember or something that a hacker can guess. For example, keeping the username as admin is a bad idea because this is one of the first options that a hacker is going to try. You should come up with something that is unique and that only you will be able to remember.

In addition, make sure that you have a good password in place. Something that is more difficult, such as a mixture of uppercase and lowercase letters as well as some numbers and symbols, will help to make it harder for the hacker to get on your site. Don't pick out words that come out of the dictionary, even if you change it up a bit, because these are easy for a hacker to get into.

Be careful with the plugins

While plugins are great tools that add to the functionality of the website that you are working on, it is a good idea to never download more than you need and get rid of the ones that you are not using. Each of these plugins come from third party developers and the more of them that are on your website, the easier it is for a hacker to get on. If you have a plugin that isn't serving much of a purpose for you any longer, that isn't activated, or it just isn't being used, it may be a good idea to get rid of it for safety.

Backup your website

It is a good idea to take some time to backup your website on occasion. This will help you out in case you need to restore it at some time because something goes wrong or a hacker gets into your information so you don't lose everything and have to start over. BackupBuddy is a good option for helping you to do this. You can also add in some plugins that ae good for helping with security overall on your website including iThemes Security and Wordfence if you are worried about someone getting onto the system.

Don't give anyone your information

Always be careful about who you are giving your information to about the WordPress site. You want to make sure that you are the only one, or maybe a few other people if you have someone who is helping to design and update the site, who are able to get onto the website. This helps to limit the amount of people who have your password and other personal information and ensures that you can keep the website going for a long time without any issues.

The security of your website should be really important to you. This is where you will often conduct your business or you need to it look professional for another reason (such as your personal portfolio or your blog). If a hacker is able to get onto the system and use that information, you will have a lot of trouble and could cause harm to your customers and your brand all at the same time. But with the right security measures, like those talked about above, you can keep your information and your website safe.

Chapter 9: Setting Up the Analytics

In this chapter, we are going to take a look at setting up some of the analytics that come with your website. It is not enough to just post up a website and leave it alone forever. There are many other websites that are out there, with businesses that are just like yours, and you want to make sure that other people, your customers, are able to find your website when they search. You want to make sure that your website is ranking high in search engines and you want to see what updates and other changes in your website will do for getting hits and searches on the site.

Before launching the website, it is a good idea to make sure that Google Analytics is all set up. This is a free tool that you can use and it is going to give you a lot of data on the visitors that are coming to your website. It is going to show you a lot of information including:

- Where the visitors to your website are coming from
- What pages do your visitors like to look through the most

- What pages the visitors are leaving the website on
- What the conversion rates are of the website

These are just a few of the things that you are able to see when you add some analytics to your website and it is going to make a huge difference on how you will conduct your business and even some of the changes that you will make to the website.

Link the website to Google Analytics

Before you can get some of the statistics that you need, you will need to get the two websites to link together. First, you must sign up for an account through Google Analytics. You can do this at the analytics.google.com website and then just follow the steps that are there to get the account set up.

During the account creation process, you should notice that there is something along the way that says "Tracking Code". This is going to start with the <script> part and then it will end with the </script> symbol. You will want to highlight this code, by holding Control (or by holding Command for the Mac) and then hit "C" in order to copy the code.

Now you can head over to the dashboard in WordPress. Hover over the plugins part before clicking on "Add New". You will not need to use this kind of plugin to link Google Analytics and your website, but we will use this method because it is better than trying to add in code to the template files

The plugin that you will need to use for this is known as "Insert Headers and Footers" from WPBeginner. Once this is installed and activated, you will need to hover over the Settings part on the dashboard and then click on this plugin. You should see that 2 boxes will come up. One of these boxes will say Scripts in Footer and the other will say Scripts in Header. Paste the tracking code that we got when we were on Google earlier and place this into the box that says Scripts in Header before clicking on Save.

Testing the tracking code

Once this tracking code has been installed into the header, you will need to wait a little bit to move on because Google Analytics will need a day or so to get this all hooked up. After this time as passed, it is time to check and see if the tracking code is working.

To see if the code is working, you will need to get

onto your Analytics account and then select the property and the view that you gave to your website. If you only added one code, you should only see one view at this time. Then you can move over to the Reporting tab before selecting on Real-Time > Overview. This is the place where you are going to be able to see a lot of the traffic that is going on for your website, in real time so you can keep up to date on who is visiting and what they are doing while on your website.

Now pull up a new tab so that you can bring up your website. Leave this tab open as you go back to your Google Analytics. You should see the words "Right Now" with a number that is right underneath it. Since you are on the website right now, you should see that there is at least 1 person under the Right Now part. This means that the code is reading it all the right way and you should be able to tell when others get onto the website as well.

If it has been a couple of days and you still can't get Google Analytics to show up the traffic that is on the site, there are a few things that you are able to do including:

- Check the code that is on your website. Get onto the website and right click anywhere. Then you can click on View Page Source. You should look at the source code and hold Control and F. Look for UA or Google.

- You can also go to gachecker.com and check out the domain name. This website will let you know whether the Google Analytics is installed on the website.

For the most part, you should not have any issues with getting Google Analytics to work on your website, you just need to give the Google page a few days to catch up and see that it is attached to your website. Sometimes beginners get excited and want to find out things right away so they get annoyed when they can't see the analytics show up after a few hours. Give it at least 24 hours before checking and everything should be working just fine.

Chapter 10: Using SEO to Optimize Your Website

Regardless of the reason that you are setting up this website, you want to make sure that you add in some of the basic marketing tools so that you can build your audience, get more people to come to the website, and to make more sales. One of the most basic marketing techniques that you can use is SEO, or Search Engine Optimization. With this technique, you will allow the search engines to crawl around and index the website without having any hiccups along the way. When this works properly, you will be able to rank higher in search results when your customers try to find you.

One thing that you should consider doing is to make sure that your customers are able to get onto your email list right from the website. The email list is going to be a really valuable asset to help you to get ranked higher in search engines.

To get started with this, we are going to install a plugin, one of the most popular ones to use in WordPress, to help out with SEO. This one is going to be Yoast SEO and it is a free one, so you will be able to find it inside of the plugin repository. The Yoast SEO plugin is going to have a lot of the features that you need to get the SEO done including analysis of your page, social integration, and technical SEO. While there is a lot of stuff that you are able to do with SEO on this plugin, we are going to keep it simple.

First, you will need to install the Yoast SEO and once you have this plugin activated, you should see that your dashboard now has a section that is called SEO. We will need to hover over the SEO and click on Social. You will need to take a moment to tell Google about your various social profiles by entering in the URLs of all these profiles. One of the main factors that Google is going to use in order to rank websites is to look at these social signals, so having this set up for you will help give some more credit to the website.

After we are done with this, you should click on Pages and you should notice on the right that there is a column that is called SEO. Each page is going to have a circle that will indicate what score it gets for SEO. Since this is a brand new plugin that you just installed, there shouldn't be a score by any of these pages because you haven't told this plugin how you want them to be graded.

We are going to go in and make some edits to just one of the pages so that we get an idea of how Yoast is going to grade it. Scroll down so you are past the text editor, and near the bottom of your page, you will see the section for Yoast SEO. This is the area that we will need to add in a focus keyword, which can help to tell Yoast what the page is about so that you can give it a grade. When we enter in the focus keyword that you want, you will be able to look at the content analysis that is right below it.

This is one of the best features that comes with this plugin; it is going to give you a full list of items that you should work on if you would like to make the page show up better on the search engines. Here you will be able to click on the button for Edit Snippet which is right about the focus keyword so that you are able to edit the SEO title, the meta description, and the slug. These are all important parts when you are working on SEO so take the time to create these well, adding in the right focus keyword that you want to use and ensuring that all of these are unique on each page.

Now if you take the time to scroll up your page a bit and look right under the heading for Yoast SEO, you will see that there are three icons and you will want to click on the 3rd icon down, the one that is the social icon, and you should notice that there are options for Twitter and Facebook. In this option, you will be able to manually change the image displayed, the description, and the title that shows up when someone posts a link to your page on Twitter and Facebook.

When it comes to SEO, this is a great feature to help you out. If you do it right, it is going to help increase how much social interaction comes on your website and search engines rank these kinds of pages really high.

You will find that there are a lot of great features that come with using the Yoast SEO plugin, but keeping up with these basics will help you to see what changes you need to make to a page to ensure that it will rank high on search engines. You can use it to make sure that each of your pages has a good description and title, that they will be unique, and that they have a good rating so that the website shows up when your customers are looking for you.

Chapter 11: Some Good Plugins to Consider for Your WordPress Website

There are so many cool things that you are able to do with your WordPress website, and part of what makes it all possible is picking out the right plugins to help your website become great. Each website is going to be slightly different depending on what you use it for and what kind of company you are, but there are some great plugins that you can use to make it easier for your customers to find you and to use your site. Some of the best plugins that you should add to your WordPress website to make it better than ever before include:

- W3 Total Cache: this is a good one to use for Web Performance Optimization. It is going to use caching with page, object, database, browser, minify, and support for content delivery network support.

- Akismet: this one is going to check some of the comments in your website against the Akismet Web service and check to see if these are spam or not. This can ensure that the customers who are commenting actually read through the information and they aren't just there to list their own websites or to cause some trouble.

- Google XML sitemaps: this plugin is nice because it is going to generate a special sitemap in XML that will help the search engines index your blog so it can be found better.

- iThemes Security: if you are looking for a plugin that is going to be good for helping out with the security of your system, the iThemes Security is one of the best ones that you can choose. It offers more than 30 ways for you to work on locking down the WordPress site. This one is easy to use and helps you to keep hackers and others off your site.

- WP Smush: this will help to reduce the size of your image files so they don't take so long to load up and it can help to speed up your SEO on the site as well as improve the performance of the whole website.

- SumoMe: this is a great plugin to use if you would like to get more email subscribers. There are some great sharing tools that will help to double your traffic through Pinterest, Twitter, and Facebook along with the other most popular social media sites.

- Backup Buddy: it is always a good idea to make a backup of your website. You never know when the website could have some issues or a hacker will get onto the website so using the BackupBuddy plugin can ensure that you will not have to start over from scratch if something goes wrong. It is a good idea to backup at least every few months so that things stay safe.

- Simple Social Icons: it is a good idea to link your website with some of your social media accounts so that your visitors are able to keep up to date on your business. This plugin is going to make it easier to add in some of the social icons that you want into the widget area on the template.

- Disable Comments: there are times when you will want to turn off all the comments on your site, such as when you don't want a discussion or you are having issues with spam on the site. The Disable Comments can make it easier to completely turn off the comments or you can make it so that you will only disable the comments based on the type of post that you are using.

These are just a few of the great plugins that you can add to your WordPress website. These will help to make it easier for your visitors to find your website and to get a really interactive experience when they come to visit you. This can make it easier to get the results that you want out of your blog or your business website, so consider adding a few of these on to make your website easier to use.

Conclusion

Thank for making it through to the end of *WordPress for Beginners: A Step-by-Step Guide to Building Your Own WordPress Website from Scratch in 2018*. Let's hope it was informative and able to provide you with all of the tools you need to achieve your goals.

The next step is to start working on your new website. If you don't have hosting or a domain name yet, that is the first thing that you will need to do, along with downloading the WordPress information from your hosting site. This makes it easy to get things started and then you can choose a theme, start writing out some of your pages for the website as well as the menu bar, plugins, and other additional things that you would like on your website. With a little bit of work, you will be able to get a professional website up and running in no time with the help of WordPress managing the site.

Creating the right website for your portfolio, your blog, or your business does not have to be difficult. Once you learn some of the tricks and tips that are available for developing your website with WordPress, you will be able to make some amazing websites in no time.

Finally, if you found this book useful in any way, a review on Amazon is always appreciated!

Search Engine Optimization 2018

The Complete Step-by-Step Guide to
Search engine optimization for Beginners

Table of Contents

Introduction

Congratulations on downloading your personal copy of *search engine optimization 2018*. Thank you for doing so.

The following chapters will discuss some of the many ways that you can optimize your website to get the best search engine rankings.

You will discover how important it is to have substantial content.

The final chapter will explore the best way to make sure that your website gets the most exposure possible.

There are plenty of books on this subject on the market, thanks again for choosing this one! Every effort was made to ensure it is full of as much useful information as possible. Please enjoy!

Congratulations on downloading your personal copy of the *name of the book*. Thank you for doing so.

Chapter 1: Ways that Google Works

Google can sometimes be difficult to figure out. This is especially true with all of the new software that is available for search engines and those who want to be able to beat the algorithms that are set up with search engines but it is important that you work to make sure that you are figuring out the right way to do things and that you are getting the most out of the Google experience.

It is also important to know that you are getting the right information. There are a lot of people who simply don't know what they are talking about and they will pass this information onto others – they either do it because they *think* they know what they are doing and want to pass it along or they do it on purpose with the intention of not letting anyone in on their secret. You want to make sure that you are doing it the right way so that you draw more traffic instead of ruining the traffic that you have and destroying your performance.

In the Past

Google's original intention was to draw people to

sites that were relevant to what they were looking for. They wanted people to see the best sites, and they came up with algorithms that would later be commonly known as crawlers that are searching the web to be able to find everything that you want to know about each of the subjects that you put into that search bar.

These crawlers weren't foolproof, though. People learned quickly that they could scam the crawlers. If they wanted those who were looking for a keyword to find them, they would just stuff their sites with a keyword. For example:

If you had a website that you wanted people who were searching for "best dog collars" to visit, you would just need to put "best dog collars" a ton of times into your site. Then, when people typed that in, you would be the first one to come up. This was a problem, though, because Google wanted people to get the most relevant results and sometimes that would lead them to scammy sites.

This practice of keyword stuffing was quickly taken care of, and Google changed its allowances to only including sites that were between 1 and 2% of the keyword that people wanted on there.

As more people figured out how to "beat" the algorithms, Google responded by having different requirements for the sites to be able to make it onto the search engine list.

Google is constantly making updates that are changing the way that people can get led to sites. After abolishing keyword stuffing, they then had to focus on backlink stuffing where sites had thousands of the same link that all led back to the same page to make the page seem more relevant. With every move that black hat search engine optimization "experts" made, Google had a counter move that allowed them the chance to make sure that they were going to be able to beat it.

This isn't to say, though, that those who practice white hat search engine optimization are able to make sure that they are getting the best experience possible from Google. People who make sure that they are doing things the right way should have no problem getting ranked. The point of it, though, is that they need to make sure that they are able to get the real idea of search engine optimization and the way that it works before they can begin to make sure that it is truly working for them. Here are the things that you will need to be able to get what you want out of Google ranking:

Trust – you need to have a trustworthy site. Have backlinks that go to legitimate other sites and content that is of high quality. The crawlers will notice.

Authority – you should be an expert or at least *look* like an expert. You should have a lot of social media followers that are reflected on your site, and you should also have a lot of information that is included on the site that is similar to the social media. You should be sharing things from your site on social media and making sure that the two are as connected as possible.

Relevance – not only do you need keywords, but you also need to make sure that they are put in your content in a way that makes sense

As long as you have these things on your site, you will be able to make sure that you are getting the best experience possible on your site

The easiest way to understand Google is that you need to have relevant keywords, but not too many. You need to have a lot of high-quality authority, and you need to be a site that is trustworthy and has been around for, at least, a year or so.

Chapter 2: The Balance of Keywords

One of the most important things that you will do when you are studying search engine optimization and learning the right way to put search engine optimization to work on your site is keyword research. This can be anything from finding what works for your site to getting the information that you need to know about each of the keywords that people are searching for right now about what your site has to offer.

You need to do keyword research because you need to have the right keywords so that the right people are led to your site – if you're selling fertilizer but people are looking for fertility help, and you use that as your keyword, there will be thousands of people who come to your site learning how to have a baby, and you'll just be selling them bags of minerals and animal dung. You will have wasted all the effort that you put into search engine optimization just to get the wrong people to your site.

You also need to make sure that you are doing the right type of keyword search for the rankings that you want. This means that you will need to be sure that you are not trying to get too high of a ranking especially at the beginning because it will be too much of a goal to try to achieve if you are not prepared for that. Even the best sites may not have the best results when it comes to keywords.

We're getting ahead of ourselves, though.

Defining a Keyword

A keyword is something that you will use for your site to define your rank in the results. This can be anything from a single world – which is the traditional definition of a keyword to a long tail keyword that has several different words in it that make up a phrase. You may be better off with long tail because it can be hard to rank (especially at the beginning) with single ones.

When you are getting started, long tail keywords will be your friend – they are easy to find, easy to do and easy to get the information for. They will also be able to help you figure out what you are doing and what is going to go on your site. The chances of ranking with a long tail keyword are much higher than ranking with a single one because of how competitive the other types are.

But, what are *Your* Keywords?

Every person who has every type of site and every reason for people to have to visit the site will have different keywords. The first step to finding your keywords is to make sure that you know what the keywords *could* be so that you will be able to start the search for the other types of keywords.

Your keywords need to be relevant. While they are long-tailed, they also need to have a relatively narrow target to them that will allow you to zone in on what you want people to visit your site for a reason. You should be specific about things. If you sell children's pajamas, you could use things like:

Buy kids pajamas
Buy kids pajamas online
Online kids pajamas
Kids pajamas for sale

These are all things that people might type in a search engine when they are looking for pajamas for their children. They will not type in something like "picture of pajamas" or "DIY pajamas" because that is not what they are looking for so try to avoid these (even if you *did* DIY these jammies)!

The Actual Keywords

If you're still lost on the keywords that you want to put on your site (which, we don't blame you – keywords are confusing), there are some things that you can do.

Steal them – the chances are that you have competitors even if you didn't know about it. Steal their keywords. As long as you don't steal their *content* (which is plagiarism, by the way), you will be just fine stealing their keywords. It is especially important to steal the ones from the competitors who are at the top of the rankings. It won't pay to steal the keywords from the ones who are on page eight of Google because the chances are that their keywords aren't great.

Make your own list – if you know some of the things that you want your people to visit your site for, you can start to make a list. The easiest way to do this is to create three different columns of things. Try to use a spreadsheet program like Excel for this. You can put words in that you will put at the beginning (like buy, purchase, where to get, get) then put the middle words (pajamas, kid's pajamas, jammies for kids, sleep pants, sleep shirts, kids PJS). Then, put the last part into it (online, high quality, custom made, cheap, cute, unique, new, USA). Add to these lists as many things that you can think of. Then, when you have about 5, at the *least,* in each of the lists, put them together in various combinations. If you have three lists (the beginning, middle, and end) with five in each of the lists, right there you will have 15 keywords that you can use. This will be long tail keywords. There will actually be more than that but it is an easy minimum number to start with.

Will Your Keywords Work?

The only way that you can find out if they will work is to check with Google. Google has options with AdWords that allow you to have a free account. From there, you can use the tools that are made for keyword planning. You can also get the "search volume and trends" button. Put your keywords into the area and then click the go button. It will allow you to see how many times the keyword got a search on Google. You should make sure that your keywords are used often and eliminate any ones that have zero hits.

Chapter 3: The Actual search engine optimization

Since you are not a web developer or a mastermind at managing the web page, the chances are that you cannot trick the search engine. That's not a good idea, anyway because Google has a huge team of specialists who are constantly trying to fight these guys and the chances are that you will not be able to use that trick for very long anyway. Instead, you should be trying to be legitimate about what you are offering on your site and the search engine options that you are putting into your site so that Google will be able to pick up everything that you have on your site.

This is where you go to make sure that Google can see you. Your site should be optimized in the best way possible to make sure that you are getting the content visible, your site allows search engines to find it, and your keywords are making their appearance in the search engines so that your site will be visible.

Your URL

This is the first place that the search engines are

going to find you. If you want people to visit a page on your site, you need to make sure that the URL is clean and that it has some of the keywords in the name of it. For example, we'll use the kid's pajamas.

Your site might automatically default to look like this: www.fakesite.com/page3/12812591?xxpage1/arti cle4551

This is messy, and it is not something that you will be able to have shown up in search engines. You should make sure that you are changing your URLS so that they look neat and clean, you can do this through your website manager, but your URL should look something like this:

www.fakesite.com/kidspajamas/girlspajamas/

This is something that will change the way that your site looks, and it will be better than trying to make sure that you are getting what you want. The results will be more likely to show up on Google, and your visitors will know exactly where they are at when they look at your site.

The Backend

The site can be set up any way that you want it to be so that you will be able to get the best results possible. Some people can make it in the way that they want, and some people choose to do it so that they can have the best search engine results – those who choose the second are the ones who have the most traffic to their site and can make sure that they are getting exactly what they need from the different options. It is a good idea to make it as easy as possible.

While some sites choose to put videos and images onto their site and then use anchor text to draw the search engines to them, there are others that simply use text on the pages that they want.

This is the best approach for you to be able to use. When you have text on your site, you will be able to show the search engines what it is all about and what is going on with your site so that you don't have to worry about trying to get the anchor text right. Google will always pick up sites more that have text that is on the actual site instead of text that is just in the form of anchor text.

Too Much or Too Little

There are some people who have started preaching not to put any keywords into a page because of the threats that come from Google on their overstuffed pages policies, but that is going to be harmful to your site – Google can't find you without, at least, a few keywords.

In general, your keyword usage should be far under 2%. It should fall somewhere between .5% and 1% but if it goes slightly over, the Google police will not come after you, and you will still be able to show up. The easiest way to do this is to design your site around a couple of keywords. This will allow you to write naturally around them and have the content that is in them. Alternatively, you can put a keyword here and there into the site to make sure that you are getting what you need. To ensure that you have the keywords weaved naturally in, always put them in the meta tags, in the headings and sometimes in the content. You will also want them in the anchor text if you are using images or videos.

You can use a site like Ubersuggest and simply copy and paste your content into it to find out what your keyword percentage is. If it is too high, just get rid of a few of the keyword instances that are within the content.

Meta Tags

We mentioned meta tags in the last little section and it is entirely possible that you froze up with that mention. New webmasters, especially those who have very little experience with Google and search engine rankings, will sometimes be confused at the use of Meta. In the simplest form possible, these are what Google displays from your site. You can design your own or let Google take care of it for you. When you design your own, you can put your keywords into it and allow yourself to be able to make sure that you are getting many more hits on your site. If you do the tags the right way, you will get more traffic. The sites that allow you to create your own site – like WordPress and Wix – will enable you to put your meta tags in. Simply look for the title information that is listed on your page in your back-office part of the website. If you use a website administrator, simply ask them if they can put the meta tags in for you and you will have them showing up in your Google results in no time.

Chapter 4: Links Matter, Too

While your keywords are important, having links on your site is nearly as important if you want to make sure that you are going to be able to get the rankings that you want. You need to have the right links on your page to show Google that you are connecting with real sites and legitimate authorities. Google knows what you are linking to and you need to make sure that you are prepared to show Google what you can do and who you are reading that is related to your site.

Different Links

There are many different options when it comes to putting links on your site. The only thing that is completely true all of the time is that you use a link that will allow you to be able to link to something that is legitimate. For example, you don't want to link to a site that has a couple of posts and a whole bunch of ads. You don't want to link to something that you have only seen once or twice, and you seriously don't want to link to a scam site.

There is a lot of debate between which type of site that is the best to link to but there is no real right or wrong in this case. Whether you are linking to an online store, a government site or a high authority blog, you will be able to enjoy the benefits that come with back linking and the information that is contained when you do the links as long as you are trying to make sure that you get all of that put into your site.

Getting Links

The easiest way to get links is to find ones on your own. Find sites that you like, blogs that are informative and government information that backs up what you are talking about. Don't link to hundreds of different things all at once or Google will kick you off of any of their rankings because that is a way to try and scam the system that was designed by Google. It is a good idea just to add links as you think of them and even design your blog posts around the links so that you can make sure that the links that you are using are the ones that are best for your site. It is always wise to find ones on your own.

Don't pay for links. Don't ask people to buy your links to your site and certainly don't buy links to other sites. The links are all accessible and all free on the Internet so just copy the links. Seriously, don't buy links. If Google finds out (and the chances are that they will), you will not be able to show up in the rankings at all. Google has policies that are in place and (even if you didn't read before agreeing) you are subject to those policies. Buying links go right along with that.

Don't Do It

Even if you find a trading link group, don't do that either. It is much easier (even if it does take longer) to try and build up the links on your site naturally so that you can have a legitimate site. There is no point in building it up fast because Google has an algorithm to figure out how fast you got those links and how much it made a difference to the way that you brought your site up. You will not show up in the results if you have not been allowed to grow your page links naturally. Trading is also against policy although it is not specifically outlined. Avoid it.

Do not pay for a network to build your links. Even though it can help you to get what you want and they may seem legitimate when you are starting out, they are scammy and spammy. They will blast your site on message boards (don't do this either, it is in bad taste). You will build your links too quickly, Google will notice, and you'll be back at zero, so you'll have to start all over again.

The Anchors

The links that you have on your site will need to have anchors to them. In general, you need to make sure that your anchor text has the information that you need to make it better optimized for your site. For example, if you are linking to a site that has information about the best materials for your kid's pajamas, you should put materials for kid's pajamas on the anchor text because it will have part of your keyword, and it will appear natural because you are not trying to stuff the whole keyword or all of your keywords into it.

Anchor text, by the way, is what you see when you look at a link. It is the clickable group of words (or single word) that you will be able to use to get to the link that the site has set up. This will allow you to make sure that you are getting what you need out of the anchors and the links. Your links will just look messy if you use the URL instead of anchor text so get used to using the anchor text every time that you do a link ... even if it is just to an image.

Chapter 5: Getting Social on Your Site

Social media is important for checking up on your high school crush and finding out when your nephew's birthday party is but it is also really important if you want to make sure that you are using the site for the best experience. There are so many options that you have with social media that will allow you to make sure that you are getting what you need out of the experience and that you are going to be able to add the different options to your site.

The point is that if you want to rank higher in the search engines, you should take advantage of social media.

Social media is used to gain traffic to your site. You need to have a social media account of some sort if you want to get the most amount of traffic and if you want to ensure that you are going to be able to get everything that you want on your site. There are many different options that you can choose from when it comes to personal social media, but when you have a business, it can be hard to manage a website as well as three or four social media accounts. Instead, focus on one.

When you feel confident with one of them, you can then move onto two.

Google Plus

The chances are that you don't use Google Plus for all of your social media needs. While the company is a technology giant, their social media platform just hasn't taken off like the company had hoped that it would. The majority of people who use + use it for business purposes and make sure that they are using it when they are trying to get higher up in the rankings for their site on Google. The company has released various statements that show they do not take this into consideration, but there is proof that having a Google Plus account will help to increase your rankings on Google. Businesses and search engine optimization experts all agree that Google *does* take it into consideration even if it is not something that they do on an official basis.

There is a good chance, though, that your competitors aren't using Google Plus because it is not quite as popular. This means that you should be using it since they don't have the advantage of that when they are doing different things with their site. Google will not rank them as high as what it is ranking you so you should make sure that you are using it in the best way possible.

Get a Google Plus account for your business (it's free!) and make sure that you add a follow button on your site.

Facebook

As the most popular social network in the world, Facebook just keeps growing and growing. What was once a simple site for Harvard students to connect with each other has grown by leaps and bounds in the years that it has been in business. Everyone uses Facebook and businesses are always making sure that they are on there and that they are relevant when it comes to the different things that are going on with the site. You should make sure that your business is working to be on Facebook and that it has *all* of the information you want.

The easiest way to make your Facebook relevant is to update it often. It is a good idea to post something about once a day. Post a link to something that is on your site every other day and is sure that you share lots of information and pictures. Like things that are from other businesses related to yours and keep the pictures updated about your business so that it has a lot of activity.

Always make sure that you have your website address is listed on your Facebook and that it is clickable. Everything that you post should have a link back to your site so that people can easily visit you.

When you are sure that your Facebook is ready to go and that you have designed it in the correct way, you will need to make sure that you are putting a "like" button on your website. This will allow people to go to your Facebook. When they like you, they will start to see your content and everything that you share (with your links) and they will then be led back to your site.

If you have both a Facebook and a Google Plus account, you will have a higher chance of getting more followers, and this will enable you to get the most amount of traffic possible. One of the great things about having both is that you will be able to post the same things to both of them. For example, you can use an app like IFTTT which stands for "if this, then that." You can set it up so that if you post to Facebook, then you will also post the same thing to Google Plus. You can even use this for several different sites that will allow you to easily manage many different social media sites at once – this is the only way that you will be able to do it without having to hire a social media manager or someone who can work specifically on that.

Your search engine optimization on social media matters, too. Make sure that you are using your keywords and that you are always back linking to your site. There are many different things that you can put on social media so make sure that you are using search engine optimization. Even Facebook uses keywords to help people find you. One thing that you *don't* want to do in the beginning is paid for Facebook advertising. Instead, use that money to help make your actual site better and get people drawn into that first.

Chapter 6: Measuring Success with Analytics

All of this will be for naught if you do not know how successful you are with the sites that you are using and the keywords that you have put onto your site and your social media. You need to keep track of how it is going and what you are doing so that you can make sure that you are as successful as possible. It is wise to make sure that you are doing well and always to check the progress that you have made so that you will not have to worry about the problems that come along with all of the options that are on your site.

Analytics will tell you what your traffic is, how much you have had come to your site and what it looks like to other people.

Google Analytics

This is the most common platform that people choose to use when they are looking at the different traffic things that are going on with their business. This is probably because most people are only worried about their Google rankings and some of the other search engines are simply not on their radar. Google makes it easy to see where you stand and to see how many people are coming to the site directly from Google. It is easy to compare what you are doing to what you *need* to be doing when you know the analytical aspect of the process.

Google Analytics will allow you to see how much traffic you have, what is going on with your site and what you need to do. It is free for Google users.

All you need to do is create an account if you don't have one or use the account that you already have on Google. If you go to google.com/analytics you can see everything that you need to about your site once you have signed up for the analytics account.

Using It

You can use the data that you get from Google to see how your site is doing and what you can improve on.

Comparison feature – Analytics allows you to compare two completely different times and dates to see what was going on with your site then. As long as you have the right URL in there, Google can see how many people came to your site, how long they stayed for and whether they clicked onto different pages with the site. It is a great way to see if people are staying and what you need to do to make sure that you are doing the right things.

The easiest comparison that you can make is a date when you first started your site to today's date. Look at the differences in the dates and then be sure that you are going to be able to get the most out of the sites and that people are visiting it. If you don't have a lot of visitors or if there is no change between then and now, you have a problem.

Charts – you can see the charts over a period, too. You don't have to just look at the two different dates that you originally compared and, instead, you will be able to figure out what is going on with your site over a period. This is great if it seems like you are having a lot of traffic and then no traffic at all. You can see the trends and then predict what is going to happen with those trends each time that you do something different on your site. As long as you are looking at the right URL, this information is accurate, and you can see if things like the season or even the time of day are affecting your traffic.

Where it Comes From

To figure out what you need to be targeting and the things that you need to do to make sure that you are getting traffic, you need to know where your traffic is coming from. You can use Google Analytics to help yourself find this so that you will be able to get the most out of the data that you have. If you want to be able to find the best information on analytics, you will need to find the acquisition section that shows you what is going on with the site and where your traffic is coming from. If it is coming from Facebook, bulk up the posts that you do on there. If it is coming from Google, add some different ads that are related to your site on there. You can choose where you are going to do paid advertising when you know what it is. Up until this point, you should not be doing any paid ads because you don't know where the right traffic is or what the right place to advertise would be.

Organics

There are many people who probably come from your site right from the search engine. These are organic clicks to the site and organic visits. Google makes sure that it has that information written down and that you can learn what you need to make sure that you are targeting the right keywords and the right people. By using the organic search information that you can find on Analytics, you can see how well your keywords are doing and what you need to do to make sure that you are going to be able to get the most out of the search engines that you are using. It is wise to make sure that you use this to your advantage and that you are going to get the most out of it when it comes to the searches that you can do on your site.

Always use the information that you find on analytics. It is a great free tool that will not only help you to improve your site but will also help you to find out what you can be doing better. It is a great tool and something that no other search engines have – Google has made it easier to figure out *how* you can improve your search engine and your rankings.

Chapter 7: Problems with search engine optimization

Now that we are quickly approaching the halfway mark of this book with all of the information that you need to know about search engine optimization and figuring out how to get your site to rank, it is a good idea to mention that there can be some problems with search engine optimization. The chances are that you already knew that, but by looking at the problems in a deeper way, you will be better prepared for them and to overcome them (or avoid them altogether).

No Listing

There is a chance that your site won't even show up on Google. That means that you are not listed, and you will not be able to make sure that you are getting the information that you need. People aren't able to find you, and you will not be able to show up when there are search engines for your keywords. Always be sure that you are doing what you can and that you are getting the best experience by showing up on Google.

Your site is probably not listed because it is new, it hasn't been shared on social media, or it does not have any content on it.

If you want to see whether you are just not showing up in the results or you are not showing up altogether, put "site:yoursitename.com" in the Google search bar. If you see any results, you are on Google but just not getting the results that you want.

No Ranking

When someone puts in a good keyword, they *could* go to your site if it is optimized. When someone puts in your site name, they *should* go to your site. Sometimes, though, you might not even rank for the name of your business. This usually only happens with sites that are brand new, so you need to let them know that you are on there.

Just link to your site. This should be done with the links on your anchor text. You can also add some other ones and then Google will be able to see that your site exists. Have some patience as it can take a while for you to be listed.

Another way that you can do this is to list your business on yellow pages, white pages, and Yelp.

This is a business listing, and it will allow you to see that you are doing it. Always link to your site when you are filling this information out. Try to find at least 50 different places where you can list your site so that you can make sure that you come up. It will work most of the time. As long as you have social media and some other links (around 50 will do the trick), you should start to see your business come up when you type in the name of your business.

Dropping Rankings

Once your site is ranking, you may think that the work is done. It is not, though. You need to make sure that you are always doing the work to get yourself ranking. If you don't, your site will begin to drop off and will not show up in all of the rankings that are available. Things that you can do to make sure that you are always able to stay on top:

- Link on social media
- Backlink to other sites
- Get your name out there
- Try some campaigns (cheap!) with ads
- Let people know that your site is out there
- Stay relevant with content – keyword rich blog posts are wonderful for this

Penalties

The chances are that, if Google is penalizing you, you are doing something that could be considered a black hat or unethical. If it happens that there is some update that is going to penalize you for what you are doing, you will have to change what you are doing and make sure that you are going to get the most out of the process. It also means that you will need to make sure that people can see your site and that you are doing everything that you can.

Try to change the things that you are doing – remember that you want to be a legitimate site, not something that is spammy or scammy for people to visit. It is important that you follow each of these things and that you always do things according to Google's policies.

If you find that you are being penalized, rewrite your site and the search engine optimization that you have on it. It will be easy to do because you'll have the framework – just make sure that you do it legitimately this time.

Building Up Your search engine optimization

There is a chance that your search engine optimization may not be ranking or may not be what you want it to be even after following each of the principles that are outlined in this book. While it is always a good idea to try things on your own, sometimes that just doesn't work, and you will have to find professional help. The best part about this is that you don't always have to pay to have a search engine optimization expert.

There are plenty of real experts that are online. As long as you stay away from search engine optimization blogs and people who tout their "perfect" methods, you can find everything that you need to know about search engine optimization on the Internet. This can be anything from the help that Google provides to WordPress and everything in between. The Wix application is designed to make your site easily optimized so try to use that to your advantage. They even have a wizard that you can follow to make sure that your site is getting the most hits and that your keywords are where they need to be –take advantage of this because it comes along with the site that you have.

Chapter 8: The Original search engine optimization – Local

The chances are that you know what businesses are and where they are located in your town because of the local search engine optimization that is used by Google to direct people to pages based on their location and the way that they are going to be able to use them. Google has created options that allow you to make sure that you are getting the things that you need from your search engines. If you have a true brick and mortar business, you should be utilizing local search engine optimization to lead people to your site so that they can find you based on their location. It is great for people who want others who are close to them to be able to find them.

The way that people search for your business in a local sense is different than organic search engine terms in that they can find you on a map. They will see your information (often with a clickable phone number), the hours that you are open and information on the quality of your business based on the reviews that other people have left about it on the same site. It is easy for people to find you, contact you and visit your website based on the local information that Google has on you.

Ranking

Just like the traditional search engine optimization and the organic search engines that you are going to be able to show up on, you will need to make some effort to be able to be seen on the search engine. This means that you will need to try to rank. There is a different course that you can take to find the way that you are going to be able to get local search results and you must make sure that you are getting what you can out of each of these when you are working your business. You should have all of this information on your site so that Google will put you up as a truly listed business:

- Address
- Google My Business information
- Location of your address
- Domain name and authority
- HTML Name
- Consistency of the site
- Legitimacy of your site and business
- Keywords that are in a title
- Business listing name
- Rates that are achieved from your rankings

If you want to be able to show up on the local

rankings for Google, you need to have these things as a minimum.

For example, if you are going to have your site listed as a physical site but someone else has something similar in the same area as you, you will need to work harder to make sure that you show up first. The chances of this happening in a big city are very high – you will almost always need to utilize search engine optimization to be sure that you are going to show up first in the rankings. In a small town with not many small business (especially if you have a specific niche), you will not have to worry about the specific competition as much as when you were doing each of the other things that are listed in that ranking.

Google My Business

This is a tool that many small businesses utilize and that you can take advantage of if you are going to be having a physical location for your business (or even if you already do). You need to make sure that you have everything that is required on the My Business page. You should make sure that you have the name of the business, the information that is required to contact you if something happens or if a customer simply wants to come to your business (these can be different numbers) and the way that you can rank according to the different sites. It is a good idea to fill this profile out completely. Always make sure that it links back to your site and that the site that is listed on your website is your homepage of the specific site that you want to be able to use.

Always choose a category that makes sense for your business. For example, if you are selling pajamas, you wouldn't want to make your category web services or anything other than clothing or retail.

Citations Are Important

Similar to how you had to list your business in directories to get your website name out there, you will need to do the same thing with your physical business and the directories that are available. In general, it is a good idea to make sure that you have around 50 different directories listing for your business. Always link all of the information for your business including your website, your phone number and any other contact information for your business. It is a good idea to try and make sure that it is listed as often as possible.

Reviews

This is another important part of the way that you can do things on your site and with your local listing. You will need to make sure that you have all of the information that you need on your site so that you will be able to get the listing done right. Having reviews will be able to help you figure out what you are going to have and will allow people to understand that you are a legitimate company.

Never pay for reviews!

The easiest way to get reviews is to ask people who have legitimately used your service for their review of the company. Have them visit your site and then have them go to Google to leave their review. It is very simple to do so if they have a Google account and it only takes a few minutes. People who are happy with your services will most likely be very willing to give you a good review. This is the only way that you will be able to get legitimate reviews that are ethical and do not go against any of the policies that are included with Google My Business.

Chapter 9: Using Schema and Microdata

There are many different sites that have information on them that people are not able to access because there is simply too much information. This is something similar to search engines but is also different in that you need to make sure that you are going to be able to show up in the different options that are included on sites.

These sites cause the search engines to crawl over them and find the information that you need to make sure that you are getting the most out of. Doing this is the easiest way for you to increase what you are doing.

It is exactly what some of the bloggers are talking about when they say that meta doesn't matter anymore. Instead, the things like microdata matter and allow people to be sure that they are going to get all of the information that they need. Microdata is different than meta in that it allows search engines to find you more easily and gives you the chance to show off the different options that you have.

Schema

The schema is a site that you can find what you need to make sure that you have the best microdata possible. It is something that all of the search engines use, and it has all of the information that you will need to be able to get the best experience possible and have all of the data that you need to put into it. There are many different meta-data problems that can be solved by using Schema. There are many ways that you can use Schema to find out the best way to put your rankings at the top.

What to Have

Since Schema is recognized by Google and is the most common thing that you can use to make sure that you are getting the information that you need, it is something that will allow you the chance to do more with your data. You need to make sure that you are following all of the information that Schema has so that you will be able to get the best markup experience possible with your microdata. You need to have the best reviews, followers, and products. Microdata will also include mentions of your site name and the other information about your business that is included with content, videos, music and even with events that are listed in various formats including with the social media mentions. It is a good idea to try and figure this out by formatting the codes.

Always add a description, the address and your business name to your information so that the code is prioritized. The Schema approach would be to show that the site has a lot of information on it and that it has a phone number and even an address. By using Schema, you will help Google to pick up on the business listing. It will simply be like reminding the spiders to pick it up as they crawl through the various information. Try to make sure that you are adding all of the data that you need to your site before you write it out so that you don't have to go back and retag anything.

Facebook

Even though Google and Bing and even Yahoo accept the coding that is implemented by Schema, there is always something that will make things more difficult for webmasters. In this case, it is that Facebook does not recognize this. It is something that will make it harder for you if you are trying to get a social following (which you should be doing) and if you have a business that is close to your area, you need to make sure that you have it listed as such.

Similar to how having a social media profile will help you when it comes to traditional search engines, it will also help you when it comes to local search engine optimization. You need to make sure that you are using the Open Graph language that Facebook recognizes so that you can be sure that you are going to make sure that you can have your business listed on Facebook. People will also be able to follow you more easily if they have everything that they need to know right there in front of them.

Use the Open Graph tool to add everything that you want to your Facebook. The main things that you should have are all of the types of your contact information. You should have the phone number to your business as well as the website where people can find you. This will allow you to see that you can do different things with your Facebook and that you can add all of the contact information that you need.

There are many people who do not have local search engine optimization because they do not think that they need it. These are mostly online businesses that do not plan to open a brick and mortar location because they do the majority of their business online, but you should still have the local search engine optimization because it will allow you to have a better chance at people coming to your site.

One thing that you can do if you want to make sure that people don't just show up at the office that you work out of is sure that you are only going to be able to be open at certain times. When you set up your Google profile and the information for your business, make sure that you put in that you are only available by appointment and that people cannot visit your business unless they have gone to your website or talked to you on the phone first. This will keep the majority of unwanted visitors away while still allowing you to have that important local listing on Google that will help to increase the traffic that you get on your site.

Chapter 10: Tools You Need for search engine optimization

Search engine optimization isn't just all about what you can do on your own. While it is beneficial to be able to do the majority of things that are on search engine optimization on your own and you can help yourself by not having to hire a professional, you will still need to use some tools.

There is no way around using the tools – they are designed for everyone who wants to do search engine optimization from the people who are professionals to novices who are just getting started with search engine optimization. This means that you will need to make sure that you are getting everything that you want and that you are going to be able to put the information up that you want on your site. There is no way to get a lot of traffic unless you use the tools that are given to you. While the majority of basic tools that you need for simply search engine optimization are free, there are some that do cost money, and you will need to figure out how to use these and what the best approach is when you are considering all of the costs of your business and your website.

AdWords Planner – you need to make sure that you are getting the right keywords. Google AdWords Planner is the best thing to being able to do this. You can find out the number of times that a keyword can be used and a number of times that you need to make sure that it is used. There are many different options that you can select when you are using this tool so make sure that you choose the one that is going to work the best for you. It is best to make sure that you know what type of traffic you want to be able to get before you use planner.

Trends – see how you can figure out the market that you have. It will allow you to adjust your information so that you can get the best rankings. When you use Trends, you will be able to find out what you need to do to figure out the way that you are doing different things and how you can control the different options that are listed in your search engine optimization ranking. It will also give you an idea to compare yourself to competitors, to your past site and the market overall.

Samurai – you can use this to help yourself figure out the basics of your keywords. It is different than AdWords in that it gives you ideas based on your site and the market, that you are a part of instead of being based on different keywords that you have put into it. It will allow you the chance to make sure that you are getting the best keywords and that you will be able to add all of the different information to it. There are many different options, and this has a free version as well as a paid version that allows you to do so much more.

Moz – the search engine optimization experts. You can find everything that you need to know about your site, the way that it ranks, your keyword and even your brand. You will even be able to get suggestions that are right on your site, and you can see how the crawlers are going to work on your site. There are, again, two version of this. The paid version of Moz offers a lot more, and you can even get some free search engine optimization classes from the site. It allows you to become certified in search engine optimization so that if you get really good at it, you can offer search engine optimization to other people and make money that way.

Analyzer – this is different than the other tools in that it looks at your site and it can see the different ways that the keywords are going to work on your site. There are many different options that you can find on here, and you will be able to see which keywords are working and which are not. Use the ones that work the best and eliminate the other ones to replace them with keywords that are going to be the best. This is especially helpful if you already have a site and just need to upgrade the search engine optimization on it to make sure that you will be able to add the different things.

Search engine optimizationQuake – you can use this to see where you stand on Google. It is easy to see it from Google, but you will sometimes have trouble finding that when you need it so make sure that you are finding the best options for yourself. There are many different ways to use Quake so be sure that you try all of the options. While you can purchase upgrades, you can get everything that you need from the free words that are listed on there.

Ubersuggest – one of the best keyword mention sites. It will show you the long tail keywords that you need. These are all based on data that is gathered from crawlers, and it will tell you that you need to make sure that you are getting the best information possible. You will also need to figure out the right way to be able to get the information downloaded. When you find these keywords, add them to your site and make sure that they are all in there in the right way – don't overstuff them. This site is also great because it allows you to see if you are using too many keywords. You can just copy and paste your content for the exact percentage of the keywords that you have. If you are over 2%, you need to rethink the keywords and try something else that will allow you to not have too many. The crawlers will not like it if you have too many keywords because it will look like you are trying to stuff it full. Use this to determine that and figure out if you have too many or too few.

Chapter 11: The Updates on Google

There is always a chance that Google will change the way that they do things. In fact, it is very likely that it is going to happen and it is something that you will need to handle when it does happen. You should always do your best to be prepared for Google to change the way that their algorithm. It is a good idea to have a site that is functional and one that is ready to be updated at any time that Google updates their rules.

As long as you are making sure that you are using white hat techniques (like the ones that are included in this book) to optimize your site, you will not need to worry about getting dropped as a result of the changes that Google is trying to make. It is a good idea to try and be sure that you are putting everything on your site so that you can make changes to it.

HTTPS

One of the most recent updates that Google did to the way that they rank things allows HTTPS sites to always come before sites that are simply HTTP.

Leading up to this, there were many sites that were simply not secure. People did not understand that because they simply figured that a site was a site – it was hard to tell a difference between HTTP and HTTPS for people who were making sure that things were working out the right way. When someone wanted to visit a site, they were at risk if it was not HTTPS.

While Google will still accept sites that are only HTTP and not have the secure S at the end of them, it will always rank the sites that have HTTPS higher than the ones that do not. This is not a problem if you do not have a lot of competitors or anyone who is trying to rank higher than you but it does become a problem when you realize that it is nearly impossible to rank above the HTTPS if you only have an HTTP site. It isn't about the fact that your site isn't secure – it is simply done because your site might *not* be secure instead of being totally secure like the HTTPS. Encryption is simple to do and just a small change that you can make. If you are using a program for your site, just change your encryption to secure so that you can make sure that you are always above the HTTP sites.

Blocking Doors

A doorway page is a page that does just that – creates a doorway that leads people to a different area. It means that you must make sure that you are going through the different things and that you are going to be able to get to the site only if you go through the doorway.

The site is usually one that is intended *just* for optimization purposes. If you have ever been to a site that tells you to "click here" to go to the "actual site" you have been to a doorway site. It is important to note that you will need to make sure that you are not using a doorway site.

Google recently made changes that allowed for the ranking to knock down doorway pages. While you can still have one and you can still rank, you will not be able to rank as high as what you once were with doorway pages. Google has done this to make sure that they are not being used for their search engine optimization efforts and that you are going to be able to include all of the different things with your site.

On Mobile

There are many instances where you will not be able to see a site on a mobile device simply because you are using a mobile device. This is because the site is not optimized for mobile viewing. Not only will you need to make sure that your site can be seen on a mobile device but you should also make sure that you are using the mobile search engine optimization techniques that are included with the different things.

Google will always rank pages higher when they can be seen on mobile and when they are also able to be done on a mobile device. You need to make sure that you are prepared for the things that come along with mobile rankings, and it is a good idea to try and make sure that you are getting each of the different things that you want with your mobile devices. There are so many options that are included with mobile viewing so be sure that you have done the best job possible to be able to include mobile devices.

While you may not necessarily get more traffic on a mobile device than you would get on a typical desktop site (which, you may get more traffic from mobile), you will be able to show up higher in the rankings if you are prepared with a mobile device. There are many different benefits that come with mobile devices so just be sure that you are using them to your advantage – in a world where nearly everyone carries a smartphone, tablet or both, your site should be prepared for people to view it on that mobile device instead of on a bulk laptop or desktop computer that they need to lug around.

Chapter 12: AdWords and Spending Your Money

AdWords is not only a way for you to make sure that you are getting everything that you need from your site but it is also a powerful advertisement tool that you can use to make sure that you are going to be able to get more views. The point of AdWords is that people can advertise their relevant products on the pages that there are search engines. Google allows businesses to purchase advertisements that other people will be able to see and it is a good idea to try and make sure that you are doing everything that you can to include the options that are listed on your AdWords.

When you want to do an ad on Google, you will need to use AdWords. This means that you will need to make an advertisement. The ad should be relevant to the keywords that people are going to search for when they want to see what you have. For example, you can put an advertisement for unique, organic pajamas that shows only when people search for kid's pajamas. You can also connect it with other categories so that you can make sure that it is only showing up when you want it to but make sure that you are doing what you can to be able to put different things on your site.

The way that AdWords works is that it is a pay per click model. If someone clicks on the ad that you have put on Google, you will have to pay for it. Until then, you do not pay to advertise. There are many different things that you can do to make sure that you have enough money to get the clicks that you want. AdWords will first ask you to set up a budget that you can use to be able to put your information in. This means that you will need to put things lie your payment method, the information that will be used to contact you and then the ad that you want.

Your Ad

The ad that Google puts on the results will look almost identical to the other search engine results except for it will be at the very top of the page. It will be something that you can see when you do a search and people will often think that it is part of the search. As long as the search is related to what you are doing, you will not have to worry about whether or not you are trying to fool your customers. Just be sure that you put the information in that you want and you will be able to have that ad listed.

126

The ad should have the information that you want people to know. It should be keyword optimized, but it should also be as natural as possible. Be sure that you have the right address for them to click on, the name that you want the ad to be and the information that you want people to see the ad.

Spending

You can and should set up your spending for your ad before you make the decision to put the ad on Google. You will need to put payment information in so make sure that you have a budget that you are going to set to be able to make sure that you are getting the most out of the ad. In general, you should expect to spend around $500 for the first ad. This is a low amount of advertising compared to traditional methods so be sure that it is what you need to do.

When you set this up, you can have AdWords cut off at the amount that you want to spend. It will stop showing the ad when you have used up all of the funds that you set aside. At this point, Google will ask you if you want to renew it or if you want to add more money to it so make sure that you are prepared for what you are going to spend in the future.

Additional Ads

You can then put additional ads on the site. Make sure that the site did well and that the ads worked out. Use the Google tools to be able to figure out if it increased your rankings and if it increased the amount of traffic that you can get to your site. If it does increase either of these things, you can make sure that you are going to get what you need out of it. This means that you should make another ad and put it on there. The chances are that it paid off more than what you were thinking and that you will be able to benefit from this process.

Don't Do It Yet

Don't jump into ads right away. You should first see if you can get traffic on your own. There are many different ways that you can get the traffic so try it on your own (the freeway) first and then if that does not work, turn your attention to the ads that you can create with Google. If you are going to add different things to the ad, make sure that you keep track of them so that you can remember it later on when you *do* decide to do the ad at the right time.

Try Different Ones

There is a chance that the same people see your ad over and over. It can be stale to them and may not make them want to click on it. To combat this, divide up your budget between two or more ads and then try to see if those are what will allow you the chance to be able to see that you are doing more. You should try to put new ads in all of the time and then see how each one performs. Tweak them until you are ready to make sure that they are all being done the right way.

Chapter 13: Looking at All search engine optimization

After reading through each of the chapters, you should be able to have a good idea of what search engine optimization should mean to your site. It is a good idea to try different things with search engine optimization and make sure that you know what you are doing. The hope is that you read this *before* you created your site so that you can apply each of these principles to your site. It is important that you do it before so that you don't have to try to change the formatting of each of the different things on your site.

Designing the Site

One thing that you should remember is that your site design does not matter quite as much as your content on your site. Your visitors will appreciate a site that is designed nicely, but they will want to be able to get to the site first. Impress the crawlers with your content and then worry about impressing the people who came to the site from the search engine. You will have much better results.

Keywords are Important

While some blogs and other people like to preach, that keywords don't matter anymore, they most definitely do. You need to have the right keywords to get the right results, and you will be able to see a huge increase in the traffic that comes to your site. If you are working to make sure that you are getting the most amount of traffic, you will be able to increase the number of rankings that you get on Google and even other search engines. Try your best when it comes to Google, and you will get the results that you need.

Make Money from Traffic

Once you have the traffic that you want, learn the right way to convert that. Just because you have a lot of people who are coming to your site doesn't mean that you are going to automatically make more money because of it. There are many different things that you need to do – including having something for sale on your site, but that is all dependent on the traffic that you get. No matter how great of a product you are selling, you won't be able to sell it if you don't have that required traffic.

Learning More

It is entirely possible to optimize your site without any further training, but you may need it if you plan to make your site the best possible. There are many different things that you can do with your site so make sure that you know what you are doing. It is a good idea to try to find out what you can do, how much you can work to make it happen and the right way to optimize your site. Keep in mind that you might need extra training if you want to be able to do your optimization in the best way possible.

Applying it All

Once you have learned everything that you can about optimization and the way that search engine optimization can help you with your website, you will be able to apply it to your site. If you see great results from it, you may consider different search engine optimization options. One thing that many people who are good at search engine optimization choose to do is either teach people or offer their optimization services to other websites so that they will be able to sell their services to people who want to get more from their sites – you can turn into the expert at search engine optimization.

Conclusion

Thank for making it through to the end of *search engine optimization 2018*. Let's hope it was informative and able to provide you with all of the tools you need to achieve your goals of

The next step is to make sure that you know the right way to optimize your site and to add that optimization to the site.

Finally, if you found this book useful in any way, a review on Amazon is always appreciated!

Made in the USA
San Bernardino, CA
23 May 2018